Conversation Magic

Conversation Magic

Improve Your Conversation Skills in One Evening

By Arlen Busenitz
www.SpeakingInfo.com

You can make more friends in two months by becoming interested in other people than you can in two years by trying to get other people interested in you.

-- Dale Carnegie
Author of <u>How to Win Friends and Influence People</u>

Contents

Introduction

Good conversation skills are essential to being successful, building relationships, and communicating effectively. Think about it. A person who can confidently carry on enjoyable conversations with people will be able to:

⇒ Make friends easily.

⇒ Improve your chance of success in business, sales, and moving up the career ladder.

⇒ Leave a great impression with people.

⇒ Feel confident.

⇒ Conquer shyness.

⇒ Be a social success.

⇒ Increase popularity.

My story

At one time I severely struggled with shyness. It was like a chain holding me back in relationships and in my career. My first month in face to face sales was a good learning experience, but I only made about ten cents an hour.

Since this was starvation wage, something had to change. Immediately, I began a journey to improve my people skills, conversation skills, and selling skills. Hundreds of hours were spent researching how to improve conversation, social, and people skills.

What I have learned has had a tremendous impact on my life and on those I have coached and taught.

What to expect

You will learn a proven step by step system to improve your conversation skills. This system is broken down into 5 principles. If you just apply one of these principles, you will experience immediate improvement in your conversation skills.

You will improve your conversation skills in one evening. Read and learn the principles and you'll experience benefits fast.

Each principle will have some practical exercises. Do these and it will help turn the principles into habits.

You will see results immediately. Just minutes after I coached an individual in one of these principles, they were able to conquer their shyness and confidently strike up a conversation. You can experience the same.

You'll learn:

⇒ How to instantly appear calm and confident with people.
⇒ How to confidently start conversations.
⇒ How to leave a great impression.
⇒ How to have a likeable personality that people enjoy being around.

⇒ How to quickly improve your conversation skills in one evening.

⇒ Become a person who people enjoy talking with.

What is your skill level?

Think of a scale of 1 to 10.

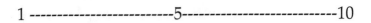

1 ------------------------5---------------------------10

If you are a 10 you are excellent at conversations, while 1 means not being very good. Where you are at? 7? 3? 5? 1? 8? It does not matter where you are, you'll learn how to dramatically improve your skills. The less your current ability, the more you can improve.

1

How to Become a Friendly Person

Who do you know that is a friendly person? Most likely it is someone who others enjoy talking with and whose personality attracts rather than repels people. Being friendly and having a good personality are essential to having good conversation skills.

I know individuals who are great at conversation in that they can confidently talk with anyone. However, because of some irritating habits, people tend to avoid them. That's not good.

Here is a simple way to help you become more friendly and likable.

Principle #1: Treat the other person as if they are the most important person in the world.

Who is the most important person in the world to you? Who is someone you consider a hero and would love to spend more time with? It could be a movie star, a family member, a special friend, or a historical figure.

If you talked with this important person, how would you respond to them in conversation? Would you treat them different than the average person? Of course.

Because they are important, you would probably:

⇒ Listen intently and not be distracted.
⇒ Show warmth and friendliness.
⇒ Portray that you are happy to be with and talking with this person.
⇒ Smile.

⇒ Ignore distractions.

⇒ Treat them with respect.

⇒ Make them the center of attention.

Your goal in conversation is to treat your conversation partner just like you would this important person. You want to consider them to be very important and to treat them as if they are the most important person in the world to you right now.

When you have this mindset, you will instantly have a more likable and friendly personality. People will enjoy talking with you. You will automatically leave a great impression.

Why this works

The basic fact of human life is that we like people who like us. We enjoy being around people who consider us important and are friendly to us. When we treat others as important, they feel important. The secret to making people like you is to make them feel important.

Respect, love, caring, and sympathy are basic qualities that we need to have when we relate with others. By treating others as a VIP, you will quickly start to display these qualities.

What does not work

What if we take the opposite attitude? If we consider ourselves more important than the other person we may treat them in the following way:

⇒ Being distracted and not listening.
⇒ Interrupting and excessively talking about ourselves.
⇒ Scanning the room for someone better to talk with.
⇒ Being unfriendly.
⇒ Frowning and not smiling.
⇒ Having an attitude that shouts, "Stay away."

How we think about the person and treat them will impact the relationship. Consider them important and you will become a friendly person.

Review & Action Plan

Principle #1: Treat the other person as if they are the most important person in the world.

Take a break from reading and walk through these steps.

Step #1: Who is your VIP (very important person) that you really respect and like?

Step #2: Find a mirror. Greet your image in the mirror just as if you were greeting your most important person. Say, "Hi." Let your face radiate you are glad to see the person. You will find that a slow smile is good. Do you appear warm and friendly? Tweak your expression and body language until you appear this way. Keep practicing this for a few minutes. The mirror will reveal how we look towards others.

Step #3: Find someone and practice treating them as a very important person. Pick up the phone, step outside your office, or talk to a clerk at the local store.

Congratulations! You are on the path to experiencing great social skills in one evening.

2

How to Overcome Shyness & Feel Confident

Do you suffer from shyness? 42% of people say they struggle with shyness. Even if you don't struggle, you may wish you had more confidence when relating with others.

Confidence is powerful. It attracts respect and makes you feel well—confident.

Many times people allow their feelings to take control. Fear, shyness, and lack of confidence direct their conversations, which can sabotage dates and other activities. This next principle is very powerful and gives instant results.

Principle #2: Act and think like a confident, friendly person.

Don't skip this principle. It is life changing. Instead of allowing feelings to control you, you'll control your actions. You'll act like a confident, friendly person. The power of this principle rests on three facts.

Three facts

> #### Fact #1
> When you are acting like a confident and friendly person you will appear like a confident and friendly person.

If you are acting confident, you will appear that way. By acting confident and great at conversation, you will appear confident and great at conversation, even though you may not feel like it.

Sound hypocritical? The majority of public speakers are battling fear and nervousness, but they refuse to let it show.

> ### Fact #2
> Acting confident and great at conversation will make you feel confident and relaxed.

William James said:

> *Action seems to follow feeling, but really action and feeling go together; and by regulating the action, which is under the more direct control of the will, we can indirectly regulate the feeling, which is not.*

Act confident and you will feel confident. Act shy and you will feel shy. This principle works.

I have seen this principle at work in classes on public speaking. A person can give a speech and do OK. However, take this same person and tell them to act, feel, and think like a confident, dynamic speaker. As they redo the speech the second time, it will look like a miracle has taken place.

- ⇒ They will be making eye contact and speaking with enthusiasm.
- ⇒ They will come across as a great speaker.
- ⇒ Nervousness will be reduced.
- ⇒ They will feel more calm and confident.
- ⇒ Their confidence draws the audience into the speech.

When I teach a public speaking class, I ask students to rate themselves on how nervous they feel. On a scale of 1 to 10, one stood for being relaxed in front of a TV and ten was losing lunch in the bathroom.

Routinely these high-schoolers would give figures of 7, 8 or even 9. On their evaluation sheets I would usually say, "You look like a 2 or a 3." This was true. They choose to act confident when they spoke, and they appeared much more relaxed than what they felt.

In addition they noticed that by acting confident, their feelings of nervousness would be reduced.

Don't worry about your feelings. Just focus on acting confident, friendly, and great at conversation.

Fact #3

The quickest way to being great at conversation is to act confident, friendly, and like you are great at conversation.

William James also said:

> *If you want a quality, act as if you already had it. If you want a trait, act as if you already have the trait.*

This is incredibly simple, but incredibly powerful. Just start acting like you are great at conversation and you will appear, feel, and be great at conversation.

How to act and think confident

Three keys will help you act and be great at conversation:

Key #1: Act confident with PRESS

In high school I created an acronym to help me remember 5 actions.

P.R.E.S.S. is an acronym that stands for:

Posture straight
Relaxed body
Eye contact
Smile
Speak clearly

By applying PRESS you will instantly act confident, look confident, and feel confident. You should use PRESS all the time.

Posture

Straighten your posture and you will feel more energetic and confident. Good posture produces confidence. It automatically makes a person look more confident.

You can have great posture by remembering or applying the following:

⇒ Stand up and place a book on your head. Adjust your posture and head until the book is balanced on top of your head. Let go of the book. When the book is balanced, your posture is straight. Now practice walking around the room with the book on your head. You will look and feel confident. It is the same exercise that beauty queens or actors will often use to straighten their posture and walk gracefully.

⇒ When standing shift your weight to the front of your feet. This automatically gives you more energy.

⇒ Walk with a purpose and don't rush. When entering a room, have your movements purposeful and confident.

Relax

The letter "R" stands for relax. As you move and sit with the right posture, practice being relaxed. Breathe. Let your arms swing at your sides. Have a relaxed look. This may seem awkward at first but practice it and you will master this ability. A couple deep breaths can also help you relax before you meet someone.

Eye contact

Proper eye contact conveys confidence and acceptance of other person. Lack of eye contact tends to show distrust and a lack of interest. Too much eye contact makes others nervous and comes across as staring.

Remember the Rule of 68. It will allow you to have effective eye contact. You will avoid the extreme of staring, yet will still display confidence.

<u>Rule of 68</u>

When Speaking: Make eye contact 60% of the time.

When Listening: Eye contact 80% of the time.

In addition keep these in mind:

⇒ Look each person in the eye when saying, "Hello."

⇒ Have a slight smile on the face to avoid scowling and staring.

⇒ Hold eye contact for an extra moment when saying "thank you" or greeting someone.

⇒ Always note the eye color when first meeting someone.

⇒ Move eyes slightly around the eye area to avoid a dead stare or glazed look.

You need to be aware of the culture and situation you are in. In the business world, increased eye contact is normal. In some cultures and areas a lot of eye contact is considered confrontational. If what I told you is making others nervous, change your style to make others more comfortable.

Smile

A smile is powerful. Studies show that smiling can put you in a good mood. Not only this, but it also radiates to others and puts them in a good mood. People with a smile are easy to approach and talk with.

Just simply smiling will make a person appear warm and friendly. Have you ever been at a social event and saw someone standing in the corner scowling? Their face is shouting stay away!

If you have a chance, look in the mirror and practice smiling. Practice smiling to greet someone. Mastering this simple ability will do wonders.

Speak clearly

You must be understood. A shy or weak voice can hinder your impression. You want your voice filled with energy and vitality. It must be warm and friendly.

The good news is that you can have an energy-filled voice in minutes. In fact, the following three steps will give you a natural energy-filled voice.

Step 1: Breathe with good posture.

A great voice starts with good posture. By transferring your weight to the front of your feet when standing, you will empower your voice with energy. The same applies to sitting. If you lean forward slightly, energy will radiate from your voice.

Often people sound weak or nervous because they are talking on little air. Taking a couple of deep breaths will calm a person down. A short sip of breath before starting to talk will allow your first words to come out clearly.

You should breathe from the abdomen. Put your hand on your stomach and breathe. You should feel your stomach moving. Often when we get nervous, we breathe from the chest. This makes the voice sound higher, weaker, and choppier. The next time you are in a nervous situation, make sure you are breathing from your abdomen.

Step #2: Open your mouth.

The voice escapes through the mouth and then heads for the ears of others. Sometimes our natural voice is squelched because we only open our mouth partway. Focus on opening the mouth and letting your voice spring forth.

An actor once told me about a great exercise for learning to speak through an open mouth. Take a pencil and place it in the mouth with the ends sticking out your mouth sideways. Keep it between your teeth. Push it as far back as possible.

Read a couple sentences and then pull the pencil out and continue reading. Repeat. The difference can be quite plain. It is training you to keep your mouth open and to project your voice. You can also use your knuckle.

Step 3: Pause and pace.

When people get nervous, they tend to talk really fast and mumble. Pace yourself and pronounce your words clearly. Pause after key points and make sure your partner has caught up with you.

If you struggle in this area, apply a simple exercise. Read a few pages from a book every day as you practice this. This will help you be aware and give you a chance to practice.

There you have it! Use PRESS as much of the time as possible. Get into the habit of always making eye contact, having the right posture, and being relaxed. You will feel confident and look confident.

A warm personality will make the other person feel comfortable in your presence. PRESS enables you to feel comfortable and confident.

Key #2: Ask yourself, "How would a confident, friendly person act in this situation?"

Think for a moment of someone who is confident, likable, friendly and great at conversation. It could be a friend, actor, movie star, or celebrity. It may be a character from a movie.

Can't think of anyone? Just imagine how a confident, likable person would act and think.

Here's a description:

⇒ Makes eye contact.
⇒ Voice is clear and does not have a hint of shyness.
⇒ Interacts with people.

⇒ Walks up to people and starts conversations.

⇒ Is relaxed.

⇒ Moves with a purpose. Not too fast, not too hesitant.

⇒ Good posture and head up.

⇒ Smile on face. No frown or negative expression.

⇒ Open body language. This means their body language communicates warmth, likeability, and openness for people to talk. The arms are uncrossed, the body is turned towards people, and there is a welcoming expression on the face.

Don't get me wrong. You are not to shed your unique personality and mimic this confident person. You are to put off any shy, unconfident mannerism like lack of eye contact, etc. Next, you put on your own set of confident, likable actions.

Whenever you are around people or are tempted to revert back to old behavior, ask this question: "How would a confident, friendly person act in this situation?" Then act that way. You will feel confident.

Key #3: Expect other people to want to talk with you and enjoy being in your presence.

Claude M. Bristol said, "We usually get what we anticipate."

Chris and Pat are both at an event. Both are acting and thinking differently:

Chris	Pat
Thinking: *I will confidently talk with people and they will enjoy being around me.*	Thinking: *No one is going to want to talk with me and I am going to say the wrong thing and look stupid.*
Gets involved in con-	Avoids conversations

| versations. | and talking with peo-ple because he is ex-pecting them to not want to talk with him. |
| Displays confidence and seems to attract people. | Lacks confidence and actually repels people. |

Your expectation is important. What you ex-pect will often happen. Why? Your expecta-tions are subtly communicated to people in your behavior. They also affect how you be-have.

When talking with people, expect them to want to talk with you. However, if they don't want to talk, let them leave.

Review & Action Plan

Principle #2: Act and think like a confident, friendly person.

Key #1: Act confident with PRESS.

Key #2: Ask yourself, "How would a confident, friendly person act in this situation?"

Key #3: Expect other people to want to talk with you and enjoy being in your presence.

Using this principle and these three keys, carry on a conversation with someone for a couple minutes. If there is no one, go back to the mirror and use the following script as you apply the three keys. It may feel weird, but it is important to apply these. You want to be a confident as you pretend to carry on this conversation:

Hello.
How are you doing today?

I am doing fine. Yesterday I, _____.
How has your week been?

Seeing yourself in the mirror will help tweak your voice and mannerism.

3

How to be Likeable and Great at Conversation

There is a secret to being great with people and dynamic at conversation. Some use it, many do not.

Charismatic people have this quality. Boring people do not.

It comes down to a person's focus and who you think about during a conversation.

Principle #3 Shine your spotlight of interest through listening and asking good questions.

Every person has a spotlight. Not a literal spotlight that lights up a dark stage, but a spotlight of interest. We can shine the spot-light on ourselves or let the other person bask in the glow of our attention and interest.

Boring people talk only about what interests them, don't pay attention, and do not give appreciation. As they shine the spotlight on themselves they may:

⇒ Avoid eye contact if it feels uncomfort-able.
⇒ Talk only about what they want to talk about and do not show interest.
⇒ Ignore the other person.
⇒ Increase their shyness because they are focusing on themselves.

If you want to leave a terrible impression, shine the spotlight on yourself. If you don't want to leave a terrible impression, shine the spotlight on the other person. It will create a dynamic conversation.

People are craving interest, attention, and appreciation. If you are giving this to them, they will enjoy being around you and you will have power in conversation.

Shining Your Spotlight

At one time I was very active in face to face sales. I attribute part of my success to the fact I showed interest in people. When I met people I asked questions. I showed interest in them. I listened. I was genuinely interested in knowing more about the person.

Interest led to quick friendships and a great impression. I have used genuine interest to talk with everyone from young kids to CEO's. The results are often the same. People enjoy the conversation and the conversation flows smoothly.

Your spotlight of interest will enable you to talk with people for hours and they will greatly enjoy the conversation.

You focus your spotlight of interest on others four key ways:

⇒ Asking sincere questions
⇒ Actively listening
⇒ Giving attention
⇒ Giving appreciation

Asking questions with sincere interest

We do not want to interrogate people or get too personal. However, people enjoy being asked questions which come from someone who is sincerely interested.

Take the question, "How are you doing?"

It can be just said as a matter of fact statement, or it can be loaded with interest. People know when a question is asked with sincere interest. They will usually bask in the glow and the conversation will flow. (Hey, that rhymed!)

Later you will learn how to use good questions. Just remember the basic concept that you want to become genuinely interested in others.

Active listening

There is a lack of good listeners. If you are a good listener, you will be likable and great at conversation.

We have all met bad listeners. The moment we start talking, their eyes glaze over. Their mind leaves the planet and eyes dart around the room.

Don't be like that! Apply these practical ideas instead.

⇒ Show you are listening. Make eye contact much of the time. Nod your head.

⇒ Pay attention to key words. Listen for key words. This will help keep your attention and give you more ammo for conversations.

⇒ Responded with short statements like, "OK. Wow! That's too bad." Also respond to what they are saying with questions.

⇒ Wait for a count of three after they finish. This will show respect to them.

Using Conversation Nuggets

When you are listening, listen for conversation nuggets. These are tidbits of information that you can show interest about or bring in your own topics.

Sarah: *We just got back from a <u>trip to Florida.</u>*
Lauren: <u>*Florida?*</u> *That sounds fun. What did you all do?*

Jerry: How was your weekend?
Tim: Not too bad. Finished up my <u>college paper</u> and <u>relaxed.</u>
Jerry: Congratulations on the <u>college paper</u>. What class was it?
Or
Jerry: That's good you had a chance to relax. I like to watch movies to relax, how about you?

Conversation nuggets are powerful. Listen for them.

Attention

When we were babies we craved attention. For the most part this has never changed. Unfortunately, people naturally try to get attention through wrong ways.

Being over-talkative, loud and boisterous, interrupting, and putting others down are just a few ways to get attention.

These methods may get attention but it sure does not make a person great at conversation or making friends!

There is a better way. Give attention and people will give it back.

> ⇒ Acknowledge them. When someone enters a circle of people, acknowledge them. If possible, nod to people as you pass them. Say "Hello."
>
> ⇒ Make eye contact.
>
> ⇒ Include people in conversation. If you are in a group, include someone

through eye contact and by bringing
them in with a question.

⇒ Listen.

⇒ Give time.

There are many ways to give attention. Focus
on doing it and it will happen. People will
bask in the glow.

Appreciation

William James said, "The deepest principle in
human nature is the craving to be appreci-
ated." Appreciation means to give value or
increase the value of something.

When people feel that we are adding value to
them or making them feeling valued, they enjoy being around us. In a sense we will be
more likable.

As a bonus we will feel good because we are
helping others out. Here are several practical

ways to shine your spotlight of appreciation on a person:

⇒ Show appreciation in your body language.

⇒ Listen and act glad to be with them.

⇒ Call positive attention to what they have done or said.

⇒ When they make a good point, say so.

⇒ Show admiration for their accomplishments.

⇒ Thank people and show appreciation.

Benefits of showing interest

When you shine your spotlight of interest, good things will happen. Friendships can be quickly made. I saw firsthand that it had tremendous power in sales.

Shyness will be conquered. Focusing on others is one the best ways to combat fears of shyness.

Review & Action Plan

Principle #3: Shine your spotlight of interest through listening and asking good questions.

1. Talk with a friend over the phone or in person. Shine your spotlight of interest through asking questions, active listening, attention and appreciation.

2. Practice listening. If you do not have a person close by, turn on the radio and listen and watch the mirror. Focus on key words. Lean forward. Pause after your conversation partner finishes.

How to Easily Start Conversations & Make Small Talk

When I coach individuals on how to ask sincere questions loaded with interest, three questions usually come up.

What questions do I ask?
How do I start the conversation?
How do I keep the conversation flowing?

Back when I was in sales, I developed a method for starting conversations and making small talk. This method is so powerful that you will be able to carry on long conversations.

Principle #4: Easily start conversations with the CQ method as you go FORTH into conversation.

Remember CQ and FORTH and you'll be able to confidently talk with anyone.

The CQ method

CQ describes two steps:

⇒ Comment
⇒ Question

You simply make a comment and then you ask a question. A comment can be virtually anything:

⇒ A greeting, "Hi."
⇒ An observation, "The weather is nice."
⇒ An expression of praise, "That is a nice car."

⇒ A story about yourself, a news story, or other interesting information.

The comment breaks the ice and lets you know if the other person is interested in continuing the conversation. After the comment, follow-up with a good conversation starter question.

Using FORTH

Questions are fuel for conversation. Asking good questions will enable you to start conversations and keep them flowing smoothly.

You will always have questions and topics when you use FORTH.

F.O.R.T.H is an acronym and gives you five categories of questions.

⇒ Family. *How are your parents? How many kids do you have? How is your health? Is your family going to be taking a vacation?*

⇒ **Occupation.** *How's work going? What do you enjoy about your job?*

⇒ **Recent events.** The most recent event is what was just said by that person. It also includes news, recent activities by both of you, etc. *Did you hear about the _____ on the news? How was the party this weekend?*

⇒ **Things.** Look around you and ask or make a comment about an item. *Nice car! Which dealership did you get it from? I noticed your English book. How are you enjoying the class?*

⇒ **Hobbies.** *What hobbies are you involved in? How did you decide to get into this hobby? How do you like to spend your time?*

Do you see the power of this? If a silent pause creeps into a conversation, quickly run through this list in your mind. You'll have instant topics.

Every situation is different, so it is hard to give blanket conversation starters. In the appendix I do list 57 conversation starters, but here are 7 good ones.

7 Conversation Starters

⟹ How is your day going?

⟹ What is new with you?

⟹ How are you enjoying this ___ (party, shopping, trip, etc)?

⟹ What have you been staying busy with lately?

⟹ How are things going in your life?

⟹ What big events are going to be happening in your life?

Memorize these and keep them on the tip of your tongue.

Two kinds of questions

Some individuals are great at asking questions, but they are asking the wrong kind.

It is essential to realize there are two kinds of questions.

⇒ Open ended questions
⇒ Closed ended questions

Closed ended questions result in just one or two word answers.

Some examples:

Do you enjoy your career? Yes.
Did you have a good day? No.
Are you enjoying the party? Yes.

Here the speaker is showing interest. However, conversations will not last long, unless the other person is a good talker. To avoid this you want to ask open ended questions.

Open ended questions result in several sentence answers.

Some examples:

How did you get started in this career?
What are you enjoying about this conference?
What's new with you?

Notice how open ended questions fuel a conversation and are a quick way to jump-start a conversation. These questions also give you key words that you can follow up on with more information.

Open ended questions are good, but don't throw away close ended questions. They are useful for gaining specific information and setting up an open ended question.

Often the follow up method is good. I will ask a closed ended question, and then follow it up with an open ended question. For an example:

Where are you going to college? Oklahoma University.
How did you decide on this college?

When I first learned about showing interest I did not understand about the two types of questions. Often I would ask only closed ended questions. It would sound like I was interviewing a person! I solved this by asking open ended questions which promoted conversation.

Review & Action Plan

Principle #4: Easily start conversations with the CQ method as you go FORTH into conversation.

You can easily start conversations with the CQ method:

⇒ Comment.
⇒ Question.

To come up with good conversation questions, remember the acronym FORTH:

Family
Occupation
Recent Events
Things
Hobbies

Take a moment to practice using these with another person.

5

How to Quickly Improve Your Conversation Skills

You've probably heard the term: *dress for success*. In other words before you venture into the workplace, on a date, or to an event, take some time to dress up, clean up, and fix up.

Experts recommend this because impressions are vitally important and people do judge you based on your dress and how you present yourself.

Take this one step further and dress for conversation success. Do this and you will notice a marked improvement in your conversation skills.

Principle #5: Dress for conversation with 5 questions and 5 topics

On a Tuesday night I took my then future wife on our first date. I wanted it to be fun and to leave a great impression. In preparation, I crafted 5 questions I could ask and also thought of 5 topics I could bring up.

Fast forward to that evening. If the conversation started to slow, I just up brought up one of the questions or topics. The result? A phenomenal first date.

Why this is important

> ⇒ You'll be less nervous knowing you are prepared.
> ⇒ You come across as being confident.
> ⇒ Your conversation will flow well because you can zap the silent pause with a question or topic.

⇒ You will increase your ability to think on your feet.

⇒ You will use the same technique the pros use.

Finding conversation topics

Conversation topics can be from the following sources:

⇒ Recent experiences that happened to you.

⇒ Any topics from FORTH.

⇒ News stories. Look at the newspaper, TV news, or an internet news site. You can use this info to ask questions about someone.

⇒ If you are a joke teller, there are different daily joke lists.

Usually I have a few news stories in mind, some personal experiences to share, interesting facts and stories.

Finding conversation questions

When you walk into a conversation, you need to be ready with around five questions. A good question will ignite conversations.

Every situation is different and you will have to tailor your questions. Below I have a few different categories of questions. Just select a few you would like to use. In the appendix there is a longer list.

Remembering FORTH (Family, Occupation, Recent Events, Things, and Hobbies) will help you think of questions.

Use the following questions to ask about topics you thought of from FORTH.

⇒ How do you like to spend your time?
⇒ What have you been busy with lately?
⇒ What do you know about _____ (Recent news item, etc)?
⇒ What is new with _____?

⇒ What do you enjoy about _____ (Raising kids, working in management, etc)?

⇒ How did you get involved in _____ (career, meet your spouse, etc)?

⇒ What do you find challenging about . . . (raising kids, your job, college, etc)?

⇒ How is your _____ (family, mother, friend)?

⇒ What do you think about _____?

⇒ Tell me about _____.

This principle will instantly make you great at conversation. Just pause to think of a few questions and topics before chatting with someone. As time passes, you will become better at this. It will automatically happen.

How to think on your feet

Have you seen individuals who can give great answers to on the spot questions? They seem to have an interesting comeback off the cuff. Do you wish you could be that way?

Many of these individuals use this secret:

> **Anticipate and formu-
> late answers ahead of
> time.**

Yes, that is the secret. Think about what kind of questions you'll be asked. Salespeople see an increase in sales when they apply this.

Anticipate what questions you may be asked and then formulate answers for them. One example is the question, "What do you do?" You know many people will ask this. Anticipate it and formulate an answer ahead of time.

Review & Action Plan

Principle #5: Dress for conversation with 5 questions and 5 topics

Think of five conversation topics and five conversation questions. With these you are ready for conversation.

How to Unleash Your Conversation Skills

You have learned five principles. Now take those and turn them into habits. Use them and you will experience the benefits. Here are two steps to help you.

Step #1: Understand that you may not be able to instantly apply all of these principles at the same time. It will take some practice. However, remember that just applying any of these principles will improve your abilities instantly.

Step #2: Review and evaluate yourself three times a day.

At each meal review the five principles. Also evaluate yourself. How well did you apply these principles? Just doing this will auto-matically help you implement them.

Step #3: Keep learning through observation and study. Check out www.Conversation-tips.com for more tips.

Review of All Five Principles

Principle #1: Treat the other person as if they are the most important person in the world.

Principle #2: Act and think like a confident, friendly person.

> **Key #1:** Act Confident with PRESS

> **Key #2:** Ask yourself, "How would a confident, friendly person act in this situation?"

Key #3: Expect other people to want to talk with you and enjoy being in your presence.

Principle #3: Shine your spotlight of interest through listening and asking good questions.

Principle #4: Easily start conversations with the CQ method as you go FORTH into conversation.

⇒ Comment
⇒ Question

Family
Occupation
Recent Events
Things
Hobbies

Principle #5: Dress for conversation with 5 questions and 5 topics

Conclusion

Just by reading this your conversation skills will have improved. As you practice and apply them you will start to see many benefits including the ability to:

⟹ Make friends easily.

⟹ Improve your chance of success in business, sales, and moving up the career ladder.

⟹ Leave a great impression with people.

⟹ Feel confident.

⟹ Conquer shyness.

⟹ Be a social success.

⟹ Increase popularity.

I would love to hear from you. Visit my site to get more conversation tips and to contact me:
www.SpeakingInfo.com

Appendix 1

Free Online Training & Bonuses

Take the next step and grab your free audio training online and extra bonuses. You'll also find links to additional information

Type in this special link:

www.SpeakingInfo.com/cmbookbonus

Conversation Magic

Appendix 2

How to Start Conversations as Easily as You Start a Car

Starting a car is easy. Put the key in, turn it, and the car starts. Would it not be great if starting a conversation was this easy? It can be – if you know how.

Unfortunately, many people don't know how. They struggle with starting conversations. If they do break the silence, the conversation sputters and dies.

This leads to boring parties, embarrassing silences, lack of friends and social skills. Not being able to easily start a conversation hinders business success and enjoyment in life. Do you know what I am talking about?

Starting a conversation can be as easy as starting a car. The reason you can quickly start a car is because you know the two steps:

Step 1: Put the key in the ignition.

Step 2: Turn the key.

These two steps work every time with virtually any car. So also there is a 2-step method for starting conversations. It will enable you to start conversation anywhere, anytime, with virtually anyone.

Step 1: Break the silence.

Step 2: Ask a good question.

Simple, is it not? Don't let the simplicity of the 2-step method fool you. It works! I have used the 2-step method with total strangers, friends, businessman, and even shy people with great success. Let me explain more.

Breaking the silence

A person cannot start a car until they put the key in the ignition, neither can a conversation start until the silence is broken. Generally, a greeting works great to break the silence.

⇒ "Hi, Tom."
⇒ "Good morning."
⇒ "Hello."

There is a second way to break the silence and that is with a comment. This works well with strangers.

⇒ On a plane: "This has been a long delay."
⇒ To a clerk: "Looks busy today."
⇒ To a friend: "That was a good football game last night."

Now that the silence is broken, it is time to get the conversation flowing with the second step.

Ask a good question

Almost any question will work. In fact any question is better than dead silence. However, a good question will get the conversation moving. Here are a few examples:

⇒ "How are you doing today?"
⇒ "How was your week?"
⇒ "What do you enjoy about this class?"

You might be thinking, "What if the conversation does not start after I ask a question?" This will sometimes happen. When it does, turn the key over again and ask another question. The conversion will eventually start.

That's it! Break the silence and ask a good question. Do this and you will be able to start a conversation as easily as you start a car.

Appendix 3

57 Questions to Start Conversations & Deepen Relationships

These questions will help you start conversations and deepen relationships. Enjoy!

1. What have you done for fun lately?
2. Did anything interesting happen this week?
3. What are you doing to stay busy?
4. How did you enter this career?
5. What are major challenges you face in parenting these two kids? (Working at this job, doing this project, etc.)
6. What books, movies, tapes, or magazines do you like? Why?
7. How do you spend most of your time?
8. If you could live anywhere where would you choose and why?
9. Who is one person who has had a lot of influence on your life? Why?

10. You look really nice, where did you get
    _____?

11. Have you seen any movies recently?
    How did you like it/them?

12. What kind of music do you listen to?

13. Ask if they saw an interesting TV pro-
    gram.

14. What sports do you play or like? How
    long have you played for?

15. What did you do this weekend (week)?

16. Have you been to _____?

17. What kind of foods do you like?

18. Where are you from?

19. Where did you go to school/college?

20. Have you read any good books lately?
    What did you enjoy about them?

21. What do you normally do for fun?

22. Do you like (an interest of yours)?

23. What place do you want to visit most?

24. If you couldn't do what you are doing
    for a living, what else would you do?

25. If you could interview anyone, living or
    dead, who would it be?

26.If you knew then what you know now, what would you have done different in your teen years?

27.If your house were on fire, your family and pets were all out safely and you could only grab 3 things to take out, what would they be?

28.What is your earliest childhood memory?

29.If you were to describe the perfect marriage in a few simple sentences, how would you do it?

30.If you wrote a book, what would it be about?

31.If you knew you'd be financially taken care of for the next year, what would you do with your time or where would you go?

32.What childhood games do you remember playing?

33.If you knew you had 24 hours to live what would you do?

34. If you could be invisible for a day, where would you go, and what would you do?

35. What are some of your greatest fears?

36. What has been the happiest day of your life?

37. If you could change one thing in the world what would you change?

38. If you could change one thing about yourself what would you change?

39. What is the most important thing in your life?

40. What is the one thing you couldn't live without?

41. What is your favorite movie of all time? Why?

42. What is your favorite book of all time? Why?

43. What is the hardest thing about being _____ years old?

44. What is the best thing about being _____ years old?

45. Describe your perfect day.

46. What job would you never want to have?

47. Who is your best friend? Why are they your best friend?

48. Would you rather mow the lawn for 8 hours or give a book report in front of 500 kids?

49. What's your favorite car and why?

50. Who would you most like to meet?

51. In what other country would you most like to live?

52. What things don't men understand about woman?

53. What things don't woman understand about men?

54. What embarrasses you the most?

55. If you could take a family vacation any place in the world, where would you go?

56. If you had three wishes, what would they be? (You're not allowed to wish for money or another wish!)

57.How do you know the host here at the party?

Want to overcome public speaking fear? Would you like to captive the audience and become a dynamic speaker?

Check out Arlen's articles, books, and programs at:

www.SpeakingInfo.com

Get more Conversation Tips at

www.Conversation-Tips.com

Made in the USA
Lexington, KY
18 July 2011